IF YOU WERE A . . .

Truck Driver

IF YOU WERE A...
Truck Driver

Virginia Schomp

BENCHMARK BOOKS

MARSHALL CAVENDISH
NEW YORK

A truck driver sees many sunrises and sunsets on the long road.

If you were a truck driver, you would haul heavy loads. You'd drive a big truck as noisy as thunder.

Fresh milk, ripe fruit, fish just pulled from the water—foods must be hurried to market. Maybe you'll haul logs across snowy mountains to the sawmill. Or cross the country to bring a load of new cars to their owners.

Wherever goods are needed, you would travel. And there would always be new adventures waiting on the road ahead if you were a truck driver.

Tractor trailers back up to the loading dock to pick up their cargo.

Engines rumbling, gears grinding, trucks arrive at the factory. They back up to the loading dock to pick up today's load.

These trucks are tractor trailers. They have two parts. The tractor holds the engine and the cab where the driver sits. The trailer holds the cargo. Tractor trailers also may be called eighteen-wheelers because—you guessed it!—most have eighteen wheels. All those wheels, plus a powerful engine, let these trucks carry heavy loads over long distances.

A forklift makes loading cargo quick and easy.

A driver cranks up the landing gear that holds the trailer in place during loading.

While the cargo is being loaded, the driver inspects the truck. Engine, tires, brakes—everything must be checked carefully to make sure it's safe for the road.

Some truckers own and drive their own eighteen-wheelers. They must keep their big machines in good condition so they can carry cargo for all their different customers. Other drivers work for trucking companies that own a fleet of trucks. Company mechanics keep these tractor trailers looking good and running even better.

Trucking company mechanics get a big rig ready to roll.

The truck cab is designed for comfort and safe driving.

Cargo loaded. Ready to roll. If you were a truck driver, you'd climb into the cab. With a roar, your tractor trailer heads for the road.

Thousands of miles to go, but you don't mind. The cab is roomy and comfortable. The wide windshield and big mirrors give a great view ahead and behind. Dials on the dashboard show the engine speed, oil temperature, air pressure—everything you need to tell how your truck is doing.

Good roads and clear weather make the trucker's job a breeze.

The citizens band radio, or CB, gives truckers some company up in the cab.

Many truck drivers fill the hours listening to music on tapes or the radio. Sometimes they use their CB radios to send messages to other truckers.

"Smokey Bear with a four-wheeler"—that's CB code for a car that has been pulled over by a police officer. "Gator in the granny"—a truck has lost a tire tread in the right lane ahead. Truckers also use their CBs to talk about the weather, traffic, accidents . . . and, sometimes, just to talk.

Smokey Bear is the trucker's name for the police who patrol the highways— better watch that speed limit!

Old friends share a laugh outside the truck stop.

After hours of driving, a trucker needs a break. If you were a long-haul driver, you might pull off the road for fuel and a bite to eat at a truck stop.

Inside the truck stop, drivers swap stories over coffee and sandwiches. Outside, big tractor trailers are lined up like a row of sleeping giants. The drivers in the trucks are sleeping, too. Most tractor cabs have a sleeping bunk. Some may also have a small sink, refrigerator, stove, even a TV.

A truck with a sleeping bunk is sometimes called a "pajama wagon."

You've traveled more than a thousand miles. At last you reach the customer waiting for your cargo. It takes a lot of skill to back up an eighty-thousand-pound tractor trailer for unloading!

Maybe you'll pick up more cargo. Or maybe you'll drive the empty truck back to the factory. You might go home to spend a few days relaxing with your family. But soon it will be time to climb back into the cab and thunder down the road again.

This truck's cargo practically unloads itself.

What happens to a load of ice cream or fresh fruit on a long haul? Special refrigerated trucks, or reefers, keep these foods cool.

Refrigerated trucks bring us fresh fruits and vegetables all year long.

To keep loads cool in trucks that aren't refrigerated, the driver sprays a shower of ice.

The temperature in a reefer's trailer can be set to a gentle chill to keep strawberries from spoiling on their trip to market. With a twist of a knob, the trailer becomes a freezer. Now the trucker can cross the country with enough frozen pizzas to stock a hundred school cafeterias for a whole month.

Flatbed logging trucks carry tree trunks from the forest to lumber mills . . .
and fresh-cut wood from mills to lumberyards.

Some cargo won't fit inside a boxlike trailer. To carry these loads, the trucker must drive a flatbed truck. Fresh-cut logs, large bales of hay, and other bulky cargo are stacked on the flatbed's flat floor. The trucker uses heavy ropes or chains to hold the load in place.

Liquid loads also need special containers. The trailer on a tanker truck is like a large, shiny can, with a special lining that makes it easy to keep clean. Some tankers carry milk or water. Others hold oil, gasoline, or other kinds of liquids. The cargo is pumped in and out of the truck through a long pipe or hose.

Traveling the highway together gives these tanker drivers company and a helping hand in case of emergencies.

An auto transport truck brings new cars to the car dealer's lot.

One of the oddest-looking trucks on the road is the auto transporter. These trucks are specially designed to carry new cars from the factories that make them to the dealers who sell them.

Cars are driven onto the auto transporter's loading ramp. Then the ramp is raised so that more cars can be loaded underneath. The cars are locked in place, and the whole contraption takes to the road like a big, noisy, runaway parking lot.

Do you like traveling and seeing new places? Can you work hard, for long hours, on your own? Then get ready to rev your engine—you could be a truck driver!

First you must go to trucking school. There you will study traffic laws, highway maps, and truck repair. You will learn how to drive a tractor trailer safely and skillfully. Soon you will thunder down the road, with a heavy load to haul and the whole country stretching before you.

At trucking school, students master the rules of the road.

TRUCKING IN TIME

Before trucks were invented, people hauled goods in wagons pulled by horses or other animals.

The first motorized trucks were built in the late 1890s. They looked a lot like the old horse-drawn wagons, except the driver used a steering wheel or lever instead of reins.

28

Most early trucks were used to deliver goods like oil, milk, or fresh fruits and vegetables. The engines ran on steam or gasoline.

In the 1930s, trucks were fitted with diesel engines. Diesel fuel is less expensive than gasoline, so trucks could carry heavy loads farther at less cost.

A TRUCKER'S EQUIPMENT

The tractor cab holds the driver's seat, steering wheel, and gearshift for changing speeds. Dials on the dashboard show speed, temperature, and other measurements. Switches let the driver control the heat and lights.

Bright safety triangles warn other drivers to steer clear of a broken-down truck.

The law requires truckers to fill out a log—a record of the distance and time they've traveled.

WORDS TO KNOW

auto transporter A truck that is specially designed to carry cars.

cab The forward part of a truck, where the driver sits.

cargo Goods that are carried by truck or other vehicle.

flatbed truck A truck with a flat cargo area, used for hauling logs, large machinery, and other loads that won't fit in an enclosed trailer.

haul To pull or carry. A "long haul" is a drive that takes more than one day.

reefer A trucker term for a refrigerated trailer.

tractor trailer A truck made up of a tractor pulling a trailer. The tractor contains the engine and the driver's cab, and the trailer holds the cargo.

Benchmark Books
Marshall Cavendish Corporation
99 White Plains Road
Tarrytown, New York 10591
Copyright© 2001 by Marshall Cavendish Corporation

Library of Congress Cataloging-in-Publication Data
Schomp, Virginia, date
If you were a— truckdriver / Virginia Schomp
p.   cm.
Includes index
Summary: Describes the training of truck drivers, the vehicles they drive, and the cargo they deliver.
ISBN 0-7614-1003-1 (lib.bdg.)
1. Truck driving—Vocational guidance—Juvenile literature. [1.Truck driving. 2.Occupations.] I. Truckdriver. II.Title.
TL230.3 .S36 2000   629.28'44'023—dc21 99-461965

Photo research by Rose Corbett Gordon, Mystic CT

Front cover: Steven Nourse

Bette S. Garber, Highway Images: 1, 10, 12, 27, 30 (bottom). Index Stock Imagery: 7, 29 (top); Henry Horenstein, 2, 13, 31; Roger Kingston. 28 (top). The Image Bank: Jeff Hunter, 4-5; Stephen Marks 8; Pete Turner, 11; Andre Gallant, 20; Tom Mareschal, 22-23; Michael Melford, 24-25; Mitchell Funk, 30 (bottom left). The Image Works: Frank Pedrick, 5 (rt); Fritz Hoffman, 6; Bob Mahoney, 9; Alan Carey, 14; Michael Greenlar, 16-17; Bruce Hands, 21; Western Star Trucks 15, 30 (top right). Dale Olson, Thermo King:18. Corbis: 28; Amos Nachoum, 19. Stock, Boston: Henry Horenstein, 26. Archive Photos: 29 (bottom).

Printed in Hong Kong
1 3 5 7 8 6 4 2

INDEX